Quick Science

(formerly titled GOT A MINUTE?)

Science experiments you can do in a minute

by HERMAN and NINA SCHNEIDER   Pictures by LEONARD KESSLER

SCHOLASTIC INC.
New York Toronto London Auckland Sydney

D0804923

ISBN 0-590-41354-6

Text copyright © 1975 by Herman and Nina Schneider.
Illustrations copyright © 1975 by Leonard Kessler.
All rights reserved. Published by Scholastic Inc.

12 11 10 9 8 7 6 5   3 4 5 6 7/9

Printed in the U.S.A.   08

Contents

Wait a minute!
Just a minute!
Take a minute!
Got a minute?

Every day you have little bits of time.
You have a minute or two.
You wish you had something to do.
In this book you will find things to make,
experiments to try.

A minute here,
A minute there,
Anytime and anywhere.

Minutes in the Morning

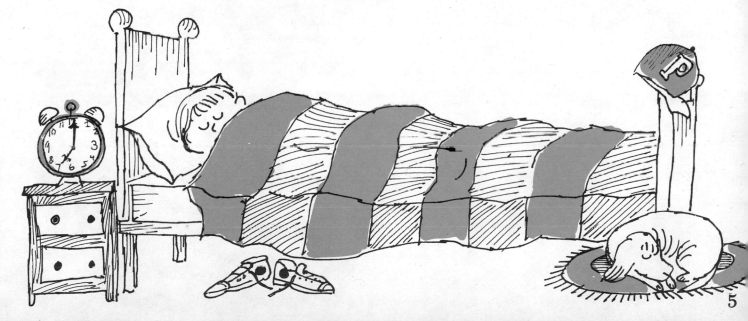

SCARE YOURSELF OUT OF BED

You don't feel like getting out of bed.
Will a skull in the air chase you out?

Look at these eyes for a whole minute.
Count like this: One Halloween,
two Halloween, three Halloween,
up to sixty. That makes one minute.

Then quickly look up at the ceiling.
There's the skull!

SCARE YOURSELF IN THE MIRROR

Hey, look! What happened here?
The eye behind the glass of water
looks bigger.
Take the glass away.
Ah! Same old eye.

7

Put your toothbrush
behind the glass.
It looks too big
to fit in your mouth!

Put the toothbrush
into the glass.
Move it back and forth.
Make it look bigger.
Make it its real size again.

Try a finger.
How fat can you make it look?

Try the toothpaste.
Read the label.
Now hold it behind the glass.
Are the letters bigger?

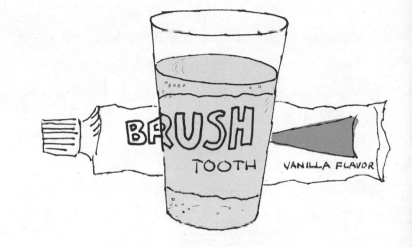

The glass is round.
The water in the glass
is held in a round shape.
The water is shaped like
a magnifying glass.
A magnifying glass
makes things look bigger.

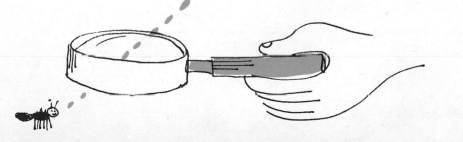

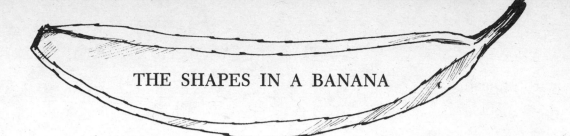

THE SHAPES IN A BANANA

Bananas are great with breakfast cereal.
They are also great for making shapes.
When you slice a banana like this
you get a shape like this.

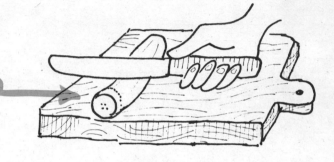

How can you get
each of these shapes?

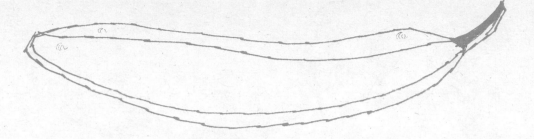

Try it.
Then eat the slices.

11

WHICH EGG IS WHICH?

Somebody made a mistake!
Somebody put some raw eggs
and some hard-boiled eggs
in the same dish.

Which is which?
You can't open the eggs to find out.
Here's the secret.

Spin each egg on a plate.
A hard-boiled egg spins well.
A raw egg spins a few times and stops.

A hard-boiled egg is solid.
It all moves together.
It spins well.

A raw egg shakes around inside its shell.
The shaking slows the egg down.
The spinning stops soon.

HOW FAST IS THE WIND?

It's a windy morning
while you wait for the bus.
You can measure the speed
of the wind while you wait.
But you need a wind-speed measurer.
Here is how to make one.

On the back cover you will
see lines with the word **Cut.**
Cut along those lines.
Fold along the lines that say **Fold.**
Put a paper clip at the end.

Now you have a wind-speed meter.
Hold it up facing the wind.
To what number does it point?
That's the speed of the wind.

If the number is 8,
the wind is blowing 8 miles an hour.
If you let a balloon go,
the wind would carry it 8 miles away
in one hour.

Here are some ways
of guessing the speed of the wind.

0 miles per hour

10 miles per hour

20 miles per hour

30 miles per hour

40 miles per hour

Quick Tricks

HOW MANY FINGERS?

Joan asks, "How many fingers
is Bill holding up?"
Tom says, "Three fingers."
Tom's eyes are closed. How does he know?

18

Tom's ear is against the table.
Joan scratches the underside of the table
three times.
The scratching sound travels easily
through wood or metal.
So Tom can hear the scratching.
But sound does not travel as easily through air.
So Bill cannot hear the scratching.

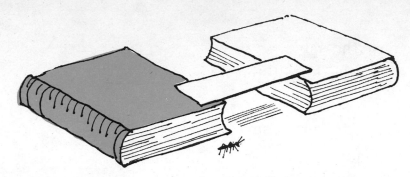

A PAPER BRIDGE

Make believe the space between the books is a river.
The books are the land on each side.
There is a paper bridge across the river.
How many coins can the bridge hold?
Guess. Ask other people to guess.

Here's the answer.
Not even one coin!

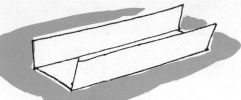

Fold the paper this way.
How many coins
can your bridge hold now?
The folded sides make the bridge stiff.
It does not bend under the load
of a few coins.

Some real bridges are made with stiff sides.

GUESS THE SHAPE

Here are some shapes.
Ask a friend to choose a shape.
Draw it on a round balloon
before you blow the balloon up.
Use a felt-tip pen.

What will the shape be
after you blow up the balloon?
Ask your friend to guess.
You guess too.
You will always guess right,
if you know the secret!

The secret is — the shape will be the same,
but it will be bigger.

Draw any shape on a round balloon.
When you blow up the balloon, it stretches.
The balloon stretches the same in every direction.
So the shape stays the same.

23

ARE YOU A BLOW-HARD NUMBER ONE?

Post card

PUT STAMP HERE

How hard can you blow?
Hard enough to lift a postcard?

24

First fold it into a shape like this.

Put it on the table and blow.
Try to make the card turn over.
Blow hard, blow easy.
Bet you can't turn the card over.

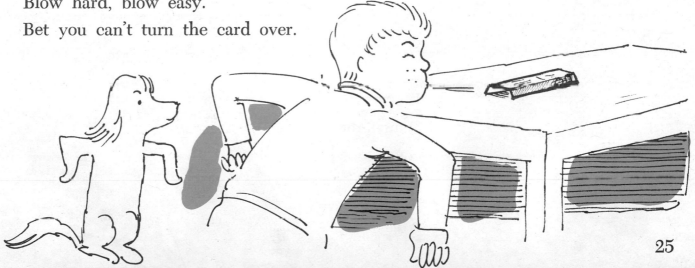

When you blow, you make air move forward.
But air also moves sideways and upward.
When air moves forward fast,
it loses some of the sideways and upward push.
There is not enough upward push
to lift the postcard!

Blow like this.
Watch the cards
come together.

ARE YOU A BLOW-HARD NUMBER TWO?

You couldn't blow hard enough
to lift a little piece of paper.
Can you blow hard enough
to lift a book?
You can if you know the secret.

Put the book on a balloon.
Blow into the balloon.
Up and over goes the book!

When you blow into a balloon
the air does not move forward very fast.
It just piles up and piles up.
Its push gets stronger and stronger,
strong enough to lift the book.

ARE YOU A BLOW-HARD NUMBER THREE?

You couldn't blow hard enough
to lift a little piece of paper.
You *could* blow hard enough
to lift a book.
Can you blow hard enough
to push the book across the table?
You can if you know the secret.

Lay the book on two soda straws.
Blow hard and away she goes!

Without the straws, the book and table
rub against each other.
The rubbing is friction.
Friction makes it hard to move the book.

The straws keep the book
from touching the table.
See how the straws turn.
They change friction into rolling.
Rolling is much easier.

Does a roller remind you of a wheel?

THE SECRET IN THE ROLLING MARBLE

There's a secret in the rolling marble!
When marble number 1
bumps into marble number 2,
something will happen.
Can you guess what?

If you roll marble number 1 faster,
something else will happen.

You can work out the secret
with five marbles and two rulers.
The rulers must have a groove
for the marbles to roll in.

When marble 1 bumps into marble 2,
the bump is passed along.
It is passed to marble 3, then 4, then 5.
Marble 5 has nothing to pass the bump to.
So it rolls.

Suppose you put marble 1
at the middle of the ruler.
What will happen? Guess and try.

Then roll marbles 1 and 2
down the ruler together.

What did you think would happen?
Did it happen?

HOW FULL IS FULL?

Here is a clean glass full of water.
If you drop a penny in,
will the water spill over?
Will it take more pennies?

Make a guess.
Take guesses from others.
If you have no pennies,
use paper clips.
Or you can use pins.

Put the pennies in carefully.
Try not to splash the water.

Somebody put in 27 pennies
before the water spilled over!
Can you do better?

Water has a kind of skin on it.
When something falls in,
the skin stretches a bit.
The water heaps up higher and higher
until at last the skin breaks.
Then the water spills over.

You could also try soapy water.
How many pennies can you put in the glass
of soapy water?

A DRYING RACE

Which will dry faster:
a wet flat paper napkin
or a wet folded paper napkin?
You can find out without waiting
for the napkins to dry.

Put the napkins on a ruler like this.
Balance the ruler on a book.
Do it at the beginning of lunchtime.
What do you think will happen?

What happened?
How long did it take?

The water dries out of both napkins.
It evaporates into the air.
The napkins become lighter.
But the flat napkin has more air around it.
So the water evaporates faster from the flat napkin.

The clothes on the line will dry faster
than the clothes in the basket.
And you know why.

Things to Make in a Minute or Two

MAKE A THERMOMETER

Did you ever see
a thermometer like this?
It has a metal coil inside.
The coil turns one way when it gets warm.
It turns the other way when it gets cold.
You can make a kind of
metal coil thermometer.

Get a piece of metal-foil paper.
It has metal on one side
and paper on the other side.
Cut a strip like this.

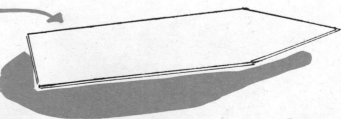

Fasten it to an empty spool with sticky tape.
Turn the strip around the spool
to make a coil.
Fasten the spool to a card with sticky tape.

Your thermometer is ready!

Take it to a cool place.
Wait a few minutes.
Make a C under the pointer.
Take it to a warm place.
Wait a few minutes.
The pointer will move to a new place.
Make a W there.

MAKE A MAGNIFIER

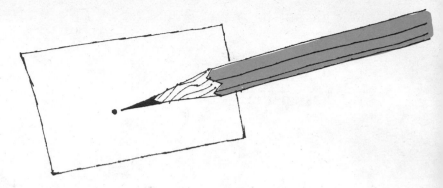

Here's a way
to make a bug look bigger —
a bug or any other little thing.
Make a pencil-point hole
in a piece of paper.

Look through the hole.
Bring the small thing close to the hole.
It looks bigger!
You have made a magnifier.

Look at some small print
and other small things.

Try it again without the magnifier.
Bring the small print closer and closer.
The print looks bigger and bigger,
but it looks fuzzier and fuzzier.

Now use the magnifier.
The small print looks sharper.

You are looking with the center
of your eye.
The center of your eye
is the part that sees most sharply.

Why did Jane put her father in the refrigerator? Because she wanted cold pop. Why did Jane put her father in the refrigerator? Because she wanted cold pop. Why did Jane put her father in the refrigerator? Because she wanted cold pop. Why did Jane put her father in the refrigerator? Because she wanted cold pop. Why did Jane put her father in the refrigerator? Because she wanted cold pop. Why did Jane

41

BE AN AIR CURRENT DETECTIVE

The air in your room is always moving.
Left and right and up and down,
the air keeps moving gently.
These movements are called air currents.

You can find the up and down currents.
First you make an air wheel.

Fold a little square of paper twice.
Then unfold it.
Cut halfway on each fold.
Bend down one corner of each piece.
Put the whole thing on
the sharp point of a pencil.

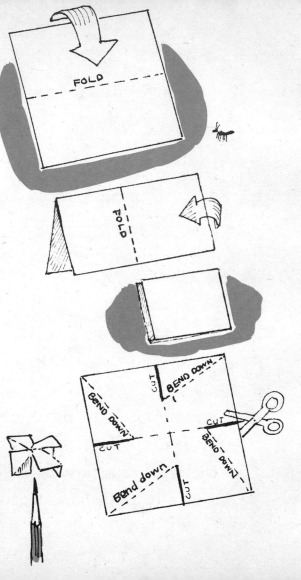

Let's look for an up current!

Hold your air wheel over a light.
The air over the light is warm.
Warm air moves up and turns your wheel.
Which way does it turn?

Now let's look for a down current.
Hold the air wheel under the bottom
of the refrigerator door.
Open the door.
The cold air comes out and moves down.
Your air wheel turns the other way.

A WATER WHEEL

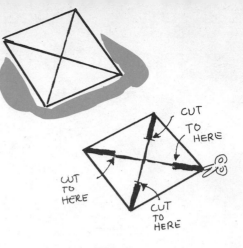

Make a little water wheel and watch it spin!
Cut a square piece of milk carton.
Draw two lines from corner to corner.
Cut halfway on each line.
Bend up one side of each corner.

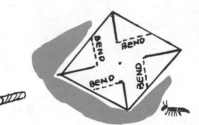

Make a pinhole in the center.
Make the hole bigger with a pencil.
Make it just big enough for a
soda straw to fit tight.
Push a piece of soda straw into the hole.

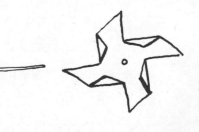

Unbend a paper clip like this.
Put it into the soda straw.
Your water wheel is ready for a spin!

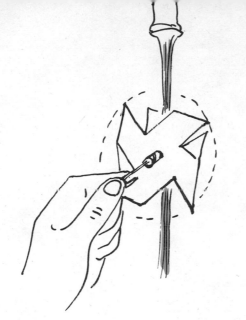

Hold the wheel in
a very small stream of water.
How does it spin?
Make the water flow faster.
The faster the water flows,
the faster the wheel spins.

In some places water wheels
are used to run machines.

Bath Time

A BATHTUB BOAT

Boats have many shapes.
Which shape is good for carrying big loads?
Do a bathtub experiment to find out.

Get a piece of kitchen aluminum foil
about the size of this page.
Get a lot of pennies or a box of paper clips.

Fold the foil like this, with
sides about one inch high.
Float your aluminum-foil boat in the bathtub.

Load it with pennies or clips,
one at a time.
How many can it carry?

Then unfold the boat and make another shape.
Make a long wide boat with low sides.
Make a short narrow boat with high sides.
Which of the three boats holds the
biggest load?

A BOAT THAT GOES BY SOAP POWER

Some boats go by wind power.
Some boats go by motor power.
You can make a boat go by soap power!

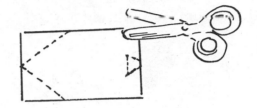

SOAP

Cut a little boat this size and shape
out of a shiny card or milk carton.
Fill the sink with cold water.
Put a tiny bit of soap on the back of the boat.
Put the boat in the water, very gently.

Watch it sail around by soap power!
Let's see how it works.

Water has a sort of skin on it.
The skin pulls from all sides.
If you put a boat without soap on water,
the boat stays still.
This is because the water skin is pulling
evenly on all sides.

But soap makes the skin weaker.
The soap is at the back of the boat.
So the pull at the back of the boat is weaker.
The pull at the front of the boat is still strong.
It pulls the boat forward.

DEEP IN THE TUB

Hold a balloon on the water.
It feels light and moves easily.
Now push it down slowly.

The deeper it goes, the harder you have to push.
You can feel the difference.
Here is a way to see the difference.

Make three pinholes in an empty milk carton.
With a ball-point pen make each hole larger.
Fill the carton with bath water.
Lift it out and look at the streams of water.
Do they look like this?
Let's see why they are different from each other.

Water falls out of the three holes.
The water at the top hole falls out because
it is pushed by the water above it.

The water at the middle hole is pushed
by the water above it.

The water at the bottom hole is pushed
by the most water.
So it comes out in the fastest stream.

The deeper the water, the more push.
Did you make the water wheel
on pages 44 and 45?
Hold it in each stream of water.
In which stream does it go fastest?

Minutes at Bedtime

SHINING YOUR PENNIES

Go to sleep with dirty pennies.
Wake up with clean pennies.

Put about an inch of vinegar in a cup.
Stir in a teaspoon of salt.
Put the dirty pennies in the cup.
Leave them overnight.

In the morning your pennies
will look like new.

SCRAMBLES

You can scramble eggs
but you can't un-scramble them.

You can scramble inks
of different colors.
Can you un-scramble them?

Get two felt-tip pens of different colors.
Make scramble marks with both pens
on a strip of paper towel.
Stand the strip in a glass.
Add enough water to reach the bottom
of the colored marks.

Look at the strip tomorrow morning.

Did this happen?

Water rises up the paper.
It carries the ink with it.
But one color of ink soaks into water
faster than the other.
And that ink is carried up sooner.

Try other colors.
Try three colors at a time.

WHAT WILL HAPPEN NEXT?

Look out for that drink!
Suppose the boy falls asleep.
The ice will melt and become water.
Will the water flow over the top?
Will the table get wet?

Try it yourself.
Fill a glass with water and ice cubes.
Leave it overnight.

Just to be safe, put a dish under the glass.

You know this about ice:
When ice melts it becomes water.

And here's something else about ice:
When it melts, it shrinks.
When an ice cube melts, the water
takes up less space than the ice cube!

When the ice cubes in the glass melted,
they all shrank.
So the water did not overflow the glass.
And nobody was wakened by drops of water
on his nose.

CAN YOU DO IT?

Here's a glass of water.
It is placed higher than the empty glass.
Can you get the water into the empty glass
without touching anything?

You can do it, but it will take a while.
You can sleep while it's happening.

BOO
SHOES

224
Brown 6½

59

What is happening?
Water soaks into the handkerchief.
It soaks up to the top and keeps going.
It goes down the other side of the handkerchief
and drips off.
When will the water stop?
Guess, and then find out.

BOO
SHOES

22Y
Brown 6½

Suppose you use muddy water.
Will the mud come up and over?
Or will just the water come over?

MAKE YOUR OWN HOT DOGS

How about a bedtime snack?
A little hot dog would be nice.
You can make one without getting out of bed.

Bring two fingertips together like this. ———→
Hold them in front of your eyes
but look at the wall.
There's a little hot dog between your fingertips!

Move your fingertips apart a tiny bit.
The hot dog is floating in the air!
But don't get out of bed for the mustard!

61

Let's see where the hot dog came from.

Your right eye and your left eye
do not see the same thing.
Hold up one finger.
Look at the wall with your left eye only.
Then look at the wall with your right eye.
Each eye sees the finger in a different place.

Now make the little hot dog again.
It's made of your right fingertip
seen with your right eye
and your left fingertip
seen with your left eye.

Good night!

Index – for adults only

Each of the activities in this book illustrates a scientific principle, phenomenon, or device. Some young scientists — and some adults — may be interested in knowing the grown-up terms for the phenomena they are witnessing.

Index